MONEY-MAKING OPPORTUNITIES FOR TEENS WHO ARE COMPUTER SAVVY

KATHY FURGANG

ROSEN
PUBLISHING®

New York

Published in 2014 by The Rosen Publishing Group, Inc.
29 East 21st Street, New York, NY 10010

Library of Congress Cataloging-in-Publication Data

Furgang, Kathy.
Money-making opportunities for teens who are computer savvy/Kathy
Furgang.—1st ed.
    p. cm.—(Make money now!)
Includes bibliographical references and index.
ISBN 978-1-4488-9388-1 (library binding)
1. Youth—Employment. 2. Money-making projects for children.
3. Technology and youth. 4. Technology and youth—Vocational guidance.
5. Internet and teenagers. I. Title.
HD6270.F867 2014
004.023—dc23

                                                        2012040037

Manufactured in the United States of America

CPSIA Compliance Information: Batch #S13YA: For further information, contact Rosen Publishing, New York, New York, at
1-800-237-9932.

CONTENTS

Tabitha has always been a computer whiz. Since she was ten years old, friends and family have been asking her for help with all things digital. One of her biggest dreams is to work at a big computer company and develop apps or computer games. But Tabitha doesn't feel the need to wait until she's an adult to get started making money using her computer skills and know-how. She is making money now as a high school student.

Tabitha is getting paid by a neighbor to transfer old home movies from reel-to-reel film onto DVD. She's also creating electronic video files for the neighbor. Those old movies will soon be able to stop collecting dust in the attic and start being compressed, stored, e-mailed, or shared with friends and family members online. Tabitha feels gratified by the work—she is having fun looking at the old videos, and she knows that the elderly neighbor would not be able to perform these tasks himself. Tabitha is offering an important service to someone who cannot afford to pay a professional digital services company to do it.

Part of the project involves adding music to the home movies. Tabitha is also including new credits and titles so that the viewer knows who appears in each scene, where the film was shot, and on what date. She is working diligently on this project because she knows that if she does a good job and her neighbor is pleased with the results, he will recommend her services to his friends and neighbors. The job is fun for Tabitha and comes easily to her. Some of the work can even be done with programs already loaded on her computer, so she doesn't have to spend any money in order to make money.

The money Tabitha earns can be put toward her college fund or simply saved for a rainy day. And the work experience

Computer-savvy teens can earn money by creating new products or helping others learn how to use their computers.

and references will look great when she lists them on a résumé or application for employment or college admission.

Many teens have the opportunity to use their computer skills to make money now, not when they are older and finished with high school or college. Whether you are a jack-of-all-trades and have mastered most computer-related tasks and activities or you have become a specialist in one particular area—like programming or graphic design—you can take steps to start earning money now.

Teens often do not realize that they have the ability to use what they already know to become their own boss now. Having the spirit of an entrepreneur is the first step to actually becoming an entrepreneur. Teens who "think outside the box" are often surprised by how easy it is to use their knowledge to make a difference in their own lives, right now. You may not have to wait until after you have finished college to start a great career. Using your computer skills to make money can help you pay for that college education. It can also help you start blazing a career path that will lead to fulfillment and success.

CHAPTER 1

WORKING FOR YOURSELF

How does someone who is computer savvy start to make money while still in high school? If you have computer and digital know-how, you will certainly be able to figure out how to make it work for you. Some entrepreneurs take a while to figure out what is right for them. You may be good at programming, design, or developing games or apps. Like Tabitha, you might enjoy working with visual media. Helping people transfer old films into a digital format or enhance their newer digital footage might be a good way to showcase your skills and earn some money. The only limits on the number of ways to apply your skills to money-making ventures are those of your imagination. If you can dream it, you can do it!

BE A TECHIE

Some small business owners or citizens in your town do not have the skills and knowledge necessary to set up, update, or sometimes even simply operate their computer equipment. People may ask you all kinds of techie questions already, so why not offer your services as a consultant to these companies or people for a fee?

A consultant works on a project basis, helping only when needed and doing the job for a predetermined price. This kind of arrangement works well for both parties involved. The company can get computer tech services when it can't afford to hire a full-time, on-site computer technician, and the consultant (that's you) gets the opportunity to use his or her skills to make money.

Computer repair can be done on a consulting basis. A consultant is paid for each individual job that he or she does for a client.

Even the average person who hires the consultant to work on a home computer would benefit from such a service. It would likely take that person a long time to learn the skills or read complex manuals that someone else may already understand. It may take a lot of time and money for someone such as an elderly person to do the work necessary to set up or update his or her computer. That person knows it is better to hire someone knowledgeable and experienced to do the job in order to avoid inadvertently doing harm to his or her home computer system through errors in procedure or mistaken actions.

Techies are often available at a moment's notice. Sometimes they may need to troubleshoot when someone has a problem. A client may not know what to do if he or she sees a certain error message on the computer screen. The consultant who is available at odd hours and can provide a reassuring demeanor can give his or her client a peace of mind.

GIVE TUTORING LESSONS

Some of the very same people who might hire a consultant to help with their tech work may wish they could learn some of the skills themselves. Taking lessons from a skilled and knowledgeable tutor can help those who are inexperienced with or intimidated by computers and other digital gadgets ease themselves into the online world (or the world of Microsoft Word, Excel, PowerPoint, Adobe Acrobat, or other programs that have them baffled).

Your clients might be older people who didn't grow up with the computer like you did. They may not be as comfortable with just diving in and experimenting with new programs.

Someone who is patient and good at explaining things might offer computer lessons or help people accomplish special tasks on the computer.

Teaching them to feel comfortable with the basics—such as universal key commands for copy, cut, paste, and undo—can make them feel more confident. Showing them how to create new files, how to organize them in folders, and how to attach them to an e-mail can make a world of difference. Sometimes all people need is someone who can work with them at their pace and answer their questions. Offering one-on-one or small group tutoring classes might be all these people need to become accomplished computer users. You may help them gain both greater independence and social connectivity.

As your students get more advanced, you can tailor the lessons to those things they really need or want to learn, such as social networking or complex design or accounting programs. You can teach them all that you know about the programs, lead them through the user guides and manuals, and direct them to user-friendly, step-by-step online tutorials.

MAKE A WEB SITE

Today, people rely heavily on the Internet and the information it has to offer. If a new business in town does not have a Web site up and running when it opens, it risks losing business. If people can't look the business up at a moment's notice to find its hours, location, and other essential information, they may very well move on to the next competitor. But not every new company has the money to pay a large Web marketing firm to design, operate, maintain, and update its Web site. A small business such as a lawyer's or a dentists' office may just need a simple Web site that you might be able to design and launch.

You may already know how to do something like this if you have made personal Web sites for yourself and your friends and family members. If you are a real techie, you can certainly do the work from scratch and use a computer language such as HTML. However, there are great Web hosting sites that do much of the work for you. Using a free Web hosting site will

Creative people can design a Web site or build an app using special programs that combine different technologies, such as film and photography.

keep your costs down, and the client will be paying you as a middleman to do the Web site's design work.

Remember that your clients are paying for your expertise so that they can spend their time focusing on what they do best—running their businesses. People with great design sense or up-to-the-minute computer skills can end up doing their client a big favor. And the job—and income—doesn't have to stop there. Web sites need to be updated regularly. Small businesses often do not have the time to do it themselves or the money to hire an employee to do it. You may be able to include updating the site in your fee or work out separate, smaller fees for updating the site after it has launched and "gone live." In addition to updating Web sites, companies may pay computer-savvy teens to update their blogs or maintain their Facebook and Twitter accounts.

MAKE AN APP

If you are full of great ideas, making apps may be for you. Some of the most popular apps available were made by individuals working alone or with only one other person. There's a lot of money to be made in iPhone and smartphone apps. Apple's iTunes store reports monthly sales of about $200 million. And there is no minimum age limit placed on those who submit apps for approval. Many of them have been made by young people, some of them still in high school. But remember that there is fierce competition. Apple receives up to ten thousand submissions every week.

So how can a mere high school student get his or her app noticed in this vast sea of competition? First, you need a great idea. Then, once you know what kind of app you want to create, you need the skill to make it work correctly. Apple says that a vast majority of the apps it rejects are turned away simply because they do not work in some way. If you have a fun, technically sound product, you can begin to cross your fingers that it gets accepted. A good-looking app that is well-designed, fun, and easy to use—and has a practical, everyday utility—will increase its chances of being promoted and featured as a new app in the App Store.

However, making an app that is accepted and made widely available does not mean that you are guaranteed to make a lot of money. Many apps are free to download, and the ones that cost money won't necessarily be bought in great numbers. The important thing is to gain recognition as a talented app designer and continue to provide consistently creative, interesting, and useful apps to bolster your growing reputation. Soon you may begin attracting attention from big-time computer and software design firms.

You do not necessarily need much experience to develop a successful and popular app. A nine-year old boy and his brother developed a math flashcard iPhone application that rose to number thirteen in the for-purchase educational app section of the App Store. They started by designing the math symbols in Photoshop, then wrote the programming code to create the game. The app cost 99 cents and was downloaded 141 times in just its first day.

BE YOUR OWN ADVERTISER

You don't have to be a programmer or super techie to make money on the computer. Someone who is digitally literate can simply use the computer and Internet to advertise other marketable skills he or she has and services offered. You can use design programs such as Photoshop to make posters, fliers, or PDFs to advertise your lawn-mowing service or availability as a dog walker or a babysitter. Try starting a Facebook page to promote your band's upcoming gig.

While you will not get paid for making your own promotional materials, you will save money that would otherwise go to a professional advertiser or designer. And, if you produce effective promotional materials, you will earn the money back by increasing the size of your client or customer base. If you were not computer savvy, you would be less effective in drumming up business for your dog walking or babysitting services.

DO SOME TOUCH-UP WORK

If you have a special knack for digital photography and computer-assisted image manipulation, storage, and sharing, you may want to think about earning money in that area. You can help people to organize and share their photo files and archive them onto discs. Or you can perform some touch-up work with the help of a program like Photoshop Lightroom. These programs can easily correct poor exposures or image imperfections, crop images, or change color images to black and white.

Offering photo services can help you make money, and it can provide a good experience for someone who is interested in a career in the arts, photography, or design. People who want this service may be neighbors or family members who just returned from a big vacation with tons of digital images. Touching up and organizing and editing family photos can be a big help to people. Working with the family members to put together a digital photo album that can later be printed as a book is another possible business idea. Small businesses may benefit from your photo touch-up work as well if they are working on their own advertising projects.

USE YOUR DESIGN SENSE

Another idea for a computer-savvy teen with an artistic sensibility is to make designs on the computer and then have them

Knowledge of graphics programs such as Photoshop is necessary for providing services such as photo retouching or creating digital family albums.

BE LIKE THE ZUCK

One of the best-known examples of young digital entrepreneurs is Mark Zuckerberg, founder of the social networking site Facebook. He was a college student when the now-famous site was launched, but it was not his first effort as an entrepreneur. He had always been a computer whiz, writing software even before entering high school. His father taught him the Atari BASIC programming language in the 1990s. He also hired a software developer to give Mark private lessons.

While still in high school, Zuckerberg took a college course to learn more about computer programming. He wrote a program that allowed all of the computers in his father's dental office to communicate with his home computers. He also wrote a music player that guessed the user's listening habits. Microsoft and AOL tried to buy the software and hire Zuckerberg. Mark was well on his way to becoming a computer-savvy success. However, he turned the companies down and enrolled at Harvard University instead. And the rest is history.

Like the founder of Facebook, Mark Zuckerberg, has shown, hard work and entrepreneurship can pay off when people have the drive and the know-how to get a job done.

printed onto T-shirts that can then be offered for sale. Using a program such as Adobe Illustrator can help you design logos or printed T-shirts for local organizations, sports teams, companies, corporate events, or charities. You can even design

T-shirts for birthday parties, wedding parties and guests, or family reunion attendees.

The possibilities are endless for promoting special events, teams, or companies in your area. While many teams or events may use professional apparel companies for their promotional T-shirt and other garment needs, you may be able to generate some business from newer groups or organizations that may not yet have a large budget for such services. Using a vector-based program such as Illustrator will allow you to scale the images to the desired size to fit on any shirt or other piece of clothing upon which you wish to print. If you don't have the equipment necessary to print the T-shirts yourself, you can use a Web site that allows you to design a shirt online and then order the T-shirts to be printed and sent directly to you or your client.

LET PEOPLE KNOW YOU ARE OUT THERE

Suppose you come up with a winning idea that you are very excited about. How can you let people know about the services that you will be offering? There are many ways to market yourself so that people know you are open for business.

WORD ON THE STREET

The safest way for young people to start finding clients is to look to those people you already know. Make it clear to people you know and trust that you are offering a particular service. Word of mouth through parents, friends, family members, and trusted acquaintances is a good way to find clients who are trustworthy and who you feel will end up paying you for your services. Once you build up a good reputation with these clients, more will quickly follow through word-of-mouth recommendations and testimonials.

MAKE A WEB SITE

A Web site is a good way to advertise your services. It does not have to be anything elaborate. If you are advertising your own Web site design services, however, be sure that your own design is a good example of the work you will be able to perform for your clients. Do a careful job and make sure all of your information is correct and any links to other sites are working correctly. When people see your attention to detail and your enthusiasm for the project, you should be able to win over some clients.

DRAFT A RÉSUMÉ

Keep track of the things you have done that make you qualified to offer the services you are providing. A résumé is a list of your special skills and accomplishments. Each project you do for a

It can take some business knowledge and networking skills to grow your income. Learn about ways that you can be paid for your services.

client is something else to add to your résumé. As you continue to make money and build a base of clients, your résumé will grow. You can hand out your latest résumé to new clients or update your old clients by letting them know how your business—and your skills and experience—have grown and evolved.

CREATE A PORTFOLIO

Collect photos, printouts, and screen grabs of any design projects you work on. These can be put into a portfolio that can help people see a sampling of the work you have done. A portfolio is a visual display of your work. Portfolios may be in book form, or they may be a digital collection put together on the computer. A digital portfolio might be showcased on a DVD or online at your professional Web site. Showing a client a portfolio can help him or her to understand the type of work you do and the quality of that work. It is a great way to drum up new business and to clarify for a client what the end product might look like. It can convince clients that you are qualified to provide them with the digital services they need.

CHAPTER
2
WORKING FOR OTHERS

You don't have to be a die-hard entrepreneur to make money with computers now. There are plenty of after-school, summer, and weekend jobs that paying employers would be happy to hire a teen to perform. Showing that you know how to use the computer and other digital tools and technologies well can give you a leg up on the competition and help you land the job. Employers are often too busy to train a person who does not already have computer skills. And more and more jobs today require a working knowledge of the computer and how several different programs work.

ELECTRONICS STORES

Someone who knows a lot about computers would be a logical choice for a computer and consumer electronics salesperson. Local electronics stores often hire young people during the summer and Christmas holiday seasons, as well as for after-school and weekend jobs.

Entry-level salespeople are given the basic information about the goods they are selling. But someone who understands the basics already—and perhaps knows far more than that—and who uses these kinds of products extensively at home and in school will be a valuable asset to his or her employer. It is not only helpful to understand computer terminology. It is also important to be able to explain complex technological concepts, capabilities, and utilities to customers who do not understand them or who are trying to decide on the best product to buy to

In computer stores like this Apple store, workers are paid on a reliable basis to offer the public their knowledge of technology and computer products.

suit their needs. Explaining the concepts and practical utility of RAM, gigabytes, modems, hard drives, memory, screen resolutions, battery life, and antivirus software can be a daunting task

for anyone. If you already understand something about processor speeds or which cables someone needs for a modem or other peripheral equipment, customers will appreciate your insight and advice.

If you do choose this line of work, it is best to be as impartial as possible and not try to sway the customer toward something that you might like for yourself. If you are partial to either the Mac or PC, the customer should not be able to tell. Your biggest concern should be to find out how the person hopes to use the computer. Then provide him or her with the computer that best suits his or her needs, whether he or she is interested in complex design programs, online gaming, video editing, or simple word processing and spreadsheets.

LOCAL AND CHAIN STORES

Have you ever been in a store and seen employees using scanners to look up inventory that might be stashed in the back storage rooms? More and more retailers are using computer technology to track goods and communicate with suppliers, their sister stores, and with customers. The people they hire to work in these stores will need a certain amount of computer expertise and training. People who can understand the technologies and perhaps even troubleshoot malfunctioning gadgets and computerized equipment could be an asset to the company and be able to beat out fellow applicants for the job. Explaining your technological abilities and interests while you are in an interview can help you to land the job.

Describing your special digital skills to the interviewer can help give you an edge over someone else who is not as computer literate. The employer is dependent on technology and computers to keep many things in the company running, from the cash registers and the store's online shopping Web site to its wedding and baby registries. Someone who is familiar with the technology and knows how to use it can hit the ground running on his or her first day on the job. He or she won't require a lot of time-consuming training during busy store hours.

An understanding of technology and computers is needed and valued in any company, including in warehouses that must keep computerized records of inventory.

DATA ENTRY

Signing up at a temporary employment agency (or temp agency) for a summer position is a good way to find job opportunities that will harness your computer and digital skills. These agencies fill positions for companies that need help on short-term projects, often during the summers or around the holidays.

One of the most common temp jobs for teens is in the field of data entry. A company may need information entered into databases collected from customer satisfaction surveys, sales figures, or mailing list forms. Once the job is finished, the worker is no longer needed, so the work is considered temporary. Some of these jobs require training in special computer software, depending on what the specific job entails.

There are many opportunities for teens to make money online in data entry jobs. However, be very cautious of these opportunities. Many are scams that require money up front from you, and then no jobs come your way. Always get permission from parents before starting any job, especially one that is offered online.

LIBRARY ASSISTANT

Almost all libraries today have computerized card catalogs. Working as a library assistant is a good way for teens to get experience with these computer databases and how they work. Once you get up to speed on the library's computerized system, you will be able to help people searching the library database to understand how the network searches work and how the card catalog system is organized.

In addition to the card catalog systems at a library, there are also computer terminals available for the public to use. The people who use these terminals often do not have a home computer of their own, so they may not have the computer skills needed to search the Internet, prepare files in word processing programs, or view CD-ROMs, DVDs, or other media on a computer. Some libraries even offer computer training courses. You may be able to help assist and instruct these library patrons.

LOCAL COMPUTER BUSINESSES

Virtually all local businesses use computers, but if you can zero in on those companies that specialize in the design or manufacture of computer hardware or software, you may be able to get a great professional opportunity that would be unavailable to your less digitally literate peers.

For example, if there is a company in your town that makes computer chips, getting a job there in any capacity can help you learn about the computer business. Even if you are working as an assistant, summer receptionist, or mailroom clerk, you will have the opportunity to see how a real computer company works, what the atmosphere is like, if

The more you know about computers, the wider your opportunities for work will be. Up-to-date computer skills are valued in just about any business.

When searching for jobs, promote your computer knowledge to prospective employers so that your skills stand out among other applicants.

the work truly interests you, and if you have an aptitude for it. An added bonus is the opportunity to talk to some of the other employees and ask them questions about their jobs, how they

got them, what they do, and if they like it. This is where you can learn new things about the industry and what it takes to begin a career. You can also meet people who may be able to recommend you for other jobs in the future.

HOW TO SEARCH FOR AND LAND A JOB

So where does someone go who is interested in finding a job that might be able to showcase his or her computer skills? The first thing to do is search local job listings. You can find these in print or online newspapers and even old-fashioned "Help Wanted" signs in the windows of businesses.

Then you must put your best foot forward. Fill out applications neatly and completely, and describe your computer skills in any blank sections of the application that allow you to talk about yourself. Explain how your particular skills can be a help to the employer. The more you know about the business and what it does, the better you may be able to shape your experience and abilities to fit what the company is looking for.

When you are called in for an interview, focus on discussing only those tasks that the job will entail. Don't steer the interviewer into talking about your computer skills if the job you applied for involves scooping ice cream or stocking shelves at a local convenience store. The computer skills should be an added bonus after the employer realizes that you would be able to adequately perform the job that was advertised.

The decisive difference between you and another qualified candidate for the job would be that you might be able to help your boss fix the computer system if it crashes. Explain that you understand how computer networks function and that

WHERE CAN THIS JOB LEAD?

The jobs you have when you are young are building blocks to your future career. The advantage of working for an employer or company—as opposed to working for oneself in an entrepreneurial enterprise—is that you can network and make good professional contacts. A boss at your first job may be able to give you a recommendation that will get you your second job. If you are working in a job that relates directly to the computer industry, you have something helpful to add to college applications or professional résumés.

Be patient about the type of job you get and exactly how it relates to your computer abilities. Remember that you are still in high school. You will have a lot of time to make digital and computer technology the main focus of your work and begin to build a career in the field.

you could help update software, or you could set things up so that the store could process credit card purchases through an iPhone or iPad, thereby reducing lines at the cash register during busy times. Remember to be honest about your abilities. Share a résumé or portfolio of your computer skills only if it is requested and/or relevant to the job you would be doing.

CHAPTER 3

GOING ABOUT YOUR BUSINESS

Not all teens make money or have jobs, so there can be a lot to learn about how to be a wage earner and a minor at the same time. Some things involve work-related laws set up by state and federal governments, such as income tax and child labor laws. Others involve getting people to take you seriously even though you are "just a kid." If you are serious about making money, it should be easy to negotiate these hurdles and come out on top.

INCOME REPORTING AND TAXES

Anyone who works for an employer, whether you are above the age of eighteen or below, must pay taxes. The federal government and most state governments require that a percentage of a person's pay go to them in the form of a tax. The taxes are used to help pay for government programs and services that keep the country in operation.

When you receive a check from an employer, taxes are already deducted from the amount you earned. If you have a personal business, however, or if you are making money doing entrepreneurial work, you will have to report the earnings to the government yourself so that it becomes aware of your income. As a result, you will owe taxes on that earned income.

If you are engaged in any independent business ventures, be sure to have an adult help you handle your money and sort out your tax obligations. Some independent workers use an accountant to help them figure out what they owe in taxes.

An accountant or other adult can help your business keep track of financial records and report income and file taxes promptly and accurately.

Some purchases you made to help you do your work—such as photo or video editing software—may be deductible from the amount of taxes that you owe. An accountant knows the latest laws and practices regarding how much money people owe—including those who are self-employed—and what their possible deductions are.

KNOWING LABOR LAWS

The United States has labor laws that are designed to help protect the rights of workers. There are laws that set the minimum age at which teens are allowed to start working, as well as the number of hours that they are allowed to work per day and per week. If you are working for an employer at a store, library, or other business, he or she should be aware of the rules regarding how many hours you can be given as part of your schedule. However, if you are creating your own business in which you are paying other teens to help you, you must be aware of any restrictions your state may have.

Many of the rules may not apply to you. But if you are interested in entrepreneurship, it is imperative to learn as much as you can about the ins and outs of owning your own business. Labor laws are an important piece of the puzzle. For example, federal labor laws restrict minors under the age of sixteen from working during school hours, before 7 AM or after 7 PM (except during the summer), or more than forty hours a week during nonschool weeks (summers and holidays). While no one will likely check on you and enforce these rules, since you are not a certified business, it helps to know for the future what laws apply to teens.

After finding out how old you must be to work in your state, you can apply for an employment certificate with your town. This will make you eligible to begin working for an employer.

USING SOCIAL NETWORKING

Social networking sites such as Facebook, Twitter, Tumblr, and Foursquare can help you promote a business or entrepreneurial idea with the expending of much less time, effort, and cash than was necessary just ten years ago. People with hundreds of friends on these sites have the opportunity to get the word out quickly about their new ideas or latest creations, services, and products.

Social networking is an important way to promote new business ventures and advertise directly to customers who might be looking for your services.

You may wish to post a picture of an iPhone app you are working on or the design for a new T-shirt you are creating. You can let people know that your services are available as a tutor or technician. You can answer people's questions right on your news feed. Explain the kind of photo and video touch-up work or digital archiving services you can offer your clients. Word may spread to others, and you may get special requests. You may even end up with potential collaborators whom you would never have imagined being able to work with otherwise.

A social networking site is also a great place to get feedback about the work you have done. Clients might thank you online so that the praise is visible to all of your other friends and potential new customers. Positive feedback is great for drumming up more business and raising awareness about your skills, knowledge, and professional services. Your online presence can help people understand exactly how much you know about all things digital, which should be very good for business.

In fact, over 1.5 million local business owners have created Facebook fan pages for their business. This is a good way to keep in contact with present and future customers and advertise to them directly—in a place where they choose to go. Fifty percent of Facebook's five hundred million users log into their accounts daily. Starting a Facebook page to advertise your business ideas and services can help you reach many potential clients and, ultimately, make a lot of money.

USING TRADITIONAL NETWORKING

Before the Internet, there was traditional, face-to-face networking. If someone needed the help of a computer expert, he or she might ask friends, family, or coworkers for recommendations. Though there was no way to instantly connect with hundreds or thousands of people to get a message or request out quickly, traditional networking worked—and it still does. If you can

Meeting people face-to-face is a great way to network, promote your business, and make new customers.

connect with people and make an impression on them, they will remember you the next time they need someone to help them.

Networking also involves making the most of your professional contacts. People you meet at work can be helpful to your career down the road. Suppose you work at a local business and you are interested in offering computer tutoring courses or computer technical assistance to people. Your boss, or anyone else you work with for that matter, can be a good source of information regarding potential new clients.

Networking works both ways. Not only will people hear about you through word of mouth, but you will also get to hear about potential clients by keeping your ear to the ground and socializing with people of all ages. If you are interested in helping people understand their own computers or network their own businesses, ask your adult family members, family friends, and friends' parents. They may know people who can use your assistance, or they may need and want it for themselves.

CUSTOMER SERVICE

Once you have found your clients, you must be sure to keep them. How can you do this? Offer services that they want, and provide them in a way that makes them happy. Customer service is a very important part of a business. It does not matter if you are working for yourself or if you are working at a big retail chain. Making a good impression and treating customers well are essential for building a good career, no matter what the field. Wear professional attire when dealing with customers, and speak in a respectful, professional manner.

You may become frustrated with people who can't quite understand the difference between a computer file and a folder, and you may want to scream and yell at them in hopes that it will finally make sense to them. But be aware that your clients are paying you to help them learn because they thought you would be someone they could rely on to teach them in a way they would understand. If you become impatient and lose your cool, you won't be making a good impression, and you will likely not be asked to help the person again. You will also blow your chance of them recommending you to their friends and family.

Customer service also involves getting back to clients in a timely manner when they contact you. When someone is having a computer problem, it could be an issue that needs to be taken care of quickly. If someone has lost files or needs

MEET YOUR PUBLIC

You've built your reputation on being computer savvy, which may very well mean that you spend lots of time in front of the computer. For many computer lovers, the thought of sitting and writing code or doing something in front of the screen is more appealing than dealing with the public or presenting ideas to potential clients. However, earning money involves some sort of interaction with others, and it could often mean working in stores or talking to the public. It is important to have a positive and energetic attitude when working with bosses, colleagues, and customers or clients.

help when a computer is acting up, you could be the calming and reassuring guide he or she so badly needs at such a stressful time.

BUSINESS ETHICS

Another important part of making money is doing things the right way. Ethics is a set of moral principles that guide a person's behavior. In other words, it means doing the right thing. In business, there is a set of unwritten rules about how to act professionally and behave properly with superiors, coworkers, those who work for or below you, and clients or customers.

When working in the world of computers, think about the ethics behind sharing for-purchase computer programs or files that are copyright protected. For instance, using a copyrighted song to provide great sound for a family's personal DVD or digital video is a good idea. But using copyrighted songs in a product that you will be selling is not a good idea. This practice

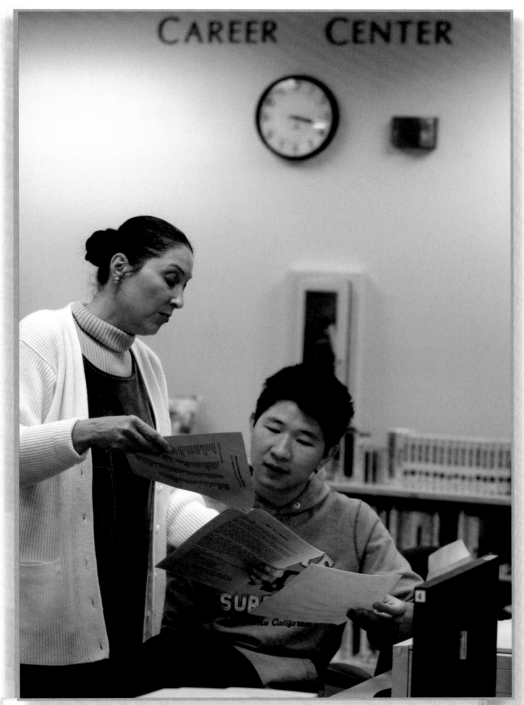

A career center can help you make sure your résumé is as strong as possible so that clients can understand the practical experience and skills you have and the services you are offering.

is unethical because it is stealing, And not only is it unethical, it is also illegal.

Another way to make sure that you are doing your best to be professional and honest is to make sure that the information on your résumé is accurate and that any samples in your portfolio are truly yours. If you worked on a project with a friend, make it clear that you did not do the work completely on your own. Similarly, be honest in interviews and try to get the job on your own merits. Don't feel the need to sugarcoat your experience or lie to make it seem like you have more experience. This will only lead to embarrassment for you when you are asked to do something you aren't yet capable of doing. And whoever hired you will be disappointed by the gap between your claims and your actual skills.

A person who hires you to provide certain services deserves to know the truth about your experiences. Chances are the person will be accepting and appreciative of what you have to say. Remember that people with hands-on professional experience and marketable skills like yours at such a young age are rare. Relax and be yourself, and people will want to hire you for who you are and the specialized work that you can do.

NAME YOUR PRICE

One of the toughest questions to answer when offering any kind of business service is, "How much do you charge?" It's not easy to answer that question because each job will be different and each client will have different needs and varying budgets. You don't want to give them a number that is too high, or they may refuse the service. If you give a number that is too low, however, you are not earning what you should for the amount of work you are putting in.

It is important to review pricing with a client before a job is started so that both parties know what to expect and are in agreement.

Pricing your work correctly may take time and trial and error. First, think about whether other teens you know provide the same services you do, and try to find out the prices they charge. It is good to be competitive with your pricing, but your fees should fall within roughly the same range as peers who offer the same services.

When you consider what to charge for your services, think about any money you have to spend up front to get the work done. Did you need to buy any new software, cables, or thumb drives to hold information? This cash outlay should be factored into the fee you charge. Make sure that the money you receive for the work will pay for anything you had to spend, while allowing you to make at least a small profit. The idea is to make money, not to spend money without being fairly compensated.

One reason that people may hire you to do computer work for them is that they assume a teen will not charge as much for the service because he or she is not as experienced as an older, working specialist. In addition, they know your operating expenses are far lower than those of a professional computer services, IT, programming, graphic design, or photo and editing company. Try looking up what a reputable company might charge for the same service you are offering, whether it be technical support, computer classes, T-shirt design, video editing, or photo retouching or archiving. Think about charging half what that company might charge so that your prices look attractive to your prospective clients.

Also think about the time you put into a job. Keep track of the hours that you have worked. Look up the minimum wage in your state to give you a good idea of the lowest amount that an employer would be required by law to pay you if you were on his or her staff. Then think about the skill level involved in what you are doing. Charge a higher price for work that requires more skill. Since you may very well be getting hired because you can do something that your client does not have the skills for, be sure to increase your price a bit to reflect that. You will be able to increase your prices as you gain more professional experience and add more jobs to your résumé.

It is important to decide with your client ahead of time how much you will be paid and the method of payment. Will you receive a check in the mail? Will someone pay you through PayPal or give you cash? How long will the client have to pay you once the work is completed? It may be best to consult a parent or other responsible adult to get his or her advice on how you should accept payment for services rendered.

CHAPTER 4
WORK NOW TO MAKE MONEY LATER

Making money as a computer-savvy teen doesn't just provide you with a little spending money or boost your college savings fund. It can also help you kick-start a career. It may not always be possible to earn money as planned, but you can always use your work experience to help build your professional future. Even though they may not earn you much money, paid and unpaid internships and volunteer opportunities can offer you invaluable compensation—actual professional experience, mentoring, networking opportunities, and a wide range of influential contacts in your field of choice.

If you are lucky enough to live in an area that has a computer services, hardware, or software company, inquire about available internships. An internship is an opportunity for people who want to learn a skill or explore a certain employment field. Internships are usually provided to students for school credit.

Many internships are undertaken on a volunteer basis, while others may offer a small payment as well as school credit. Internships are often organized programs that a student follows so that he or she can learn about different aspects of a professional field, as well as how companies are organized and structured. Internships are often offered by companies because they know that training young people for a future in the computer industry can benefit them in the long run. It also allows them to increase their manpower at little or no additional cost.

This high school intern works in his school district's finance department on a Web-based computer program. He earns school credit as well as valuable experience.

COMPUTER COMPANIES

It seems like a dream job for a computer-savvy person would be to work at a company that makes computers and hardware, software, or other digital and computer-related applications and accessories. These companies are not located in every town and

Working at a computer company in any capacity, even on an assembly line, may make it possible to move to other positions within the company at some point in the future.

community in the country, so consider yourself lucky if you have one of these companies near you.

Some companies provide state-of-the-art facilities that develop the latest computers. As an intern, you might be exposed to the design department, hardware development, or the prototype development and testing departments. Keep in

mind that some departments in a computer company may be working on confidential material that interns will not be allowed to work on or even see. However, you will still be able to learn a lot about how the company works, the products that are developed, and the range of jobs available. You can ask questions about the training people need to obtain and perform these jobs.

Computer engineers work in this field, and they work on developing computer systems and creating and analyzing software. To do this highly technical work, these people have degrees in computer engineering. They must also stay on top of changes in the industry and be informed about their competitors' products.

IT FOR COMMUNITY-BASED PROJECTS

Just about every company and large retail establishment has an information technology, or IT, department. This is where the expertise of computer-savvy employees is really put to the test, solving any of the bewildering number of computer-related problems that can crop up during a typical business day.

CHOOSE A MENTOR

One of the biggest perks of working in an internship or volunteer position is the chance to meet someone who can be a mentor to you. A mentor is someone who knows a lot about a topic or field of study. He or she can take the time to show you the ropes and explain to you how things work. A mentor may be a supervisor in a computer department or someone whom you are assigned to work directly with on a special project.

A mentor can help you learn about ways the computer world is changing and what jobs will be most in demand in the future. He or she can also tell you about job openings and recommend you for interviews and positions.

Ask a lot of questions about the job you are in. There will be many things about the computer industry that you do not know. A mentor can help open your eyes to aspects of the industry that you may not have even known existed. What's even better is that the mentor can provide information about what the best colleges are for computer science majors and what kinds of jobs those people tend to get after they graduate. A mentor is also a great person to ask for a recommendation when you need references for a job or college application.

Providing technical support to employees is a crucial job that IT departments perform. When employees need help learning new database systems or updating software, they call the IT department. When employees' computers crash, they lose important files or e-mails, or they are confused by a program they are working with, it is the IT department's job to solve the problem.

Sometimes training courses are developed by IT departments so that employees can learn how to use a new program, operating system, or database. The IT professionals have a wide range of knowledge of computers, networking, programming, and solving difficult problems related to hardware and software.

The work done by IT departments in big companies must be done on a smaller scale for community programs, nonprofit organizations, local charities, churches, and special events. These all use computers and digital information technology as part of their day-to-day operations or marketing efforts. Since many of these types of organizations have very small and constrained budgets, they would probably welcome the volunteering of your time, expertise, and digital-savvy services.

Volunteering is an important way to gain knowledge and experience and to see if you enjoy doing a certain aspect of

Volunteering in a school or library computer lab is a great way to earn valuable and practical work experience that will attract employers in the future.

computer work. For example, if one of your friend's parents is starting a new business but does not have the money to hire someone to hook up a computer network or to write code for a simple database, you can offer a hand and see how the work suits you. That work experience will look great on a résumé when you go to a local charity or church in hopes of helping it do the same thing. Training volunteers to learn a computer program for a special event is another good way to earn valuable experience. School computer labs often have student volunteers helping them to maintain their networks and assist students who need help with computer basics. This kind of work can be rewarded with class credits or extra credit opportunities.

Although a volunteer or internship experience does not translate into money right now, it can definitely be an important stepping-stone to great career opportunities in the future. That's the most important part about getting into computer work as a teen. It is a building block for the future. Not only can it help you understand the structure of some companies and the work that computer experts do, but it allows you to meet people who might be able to help get your career started after college.

CAREER BUILDING BLOCKS

Someone who is determined and energetic enough to start his or her own business or make money with computers as a teenager will know that getting what you want takes a lot of hard work. If you are ready to put in that extra effort, there is a lot you can do to learn more about computers and digital technology. By doing so, you can make yourself valuable to a future employer—even if that future employer is yourself. Here are some important tips that can help you get a leg up on the competition.

LEARNING THE LANGUAGE

Learning about computers and digital technology is a job that's never done. There's always more to learn, and there's always something new being developed that you will need to become familiar with. Computer classes are a good way to learn more and stay on top of the latest developments in the field. There are great computer classes that are open to teens that can be taken at local community colleges and trade or technical schools, high schools, or even community centers.

Computer programming is an extremely valuable skill to possess, and there are many computer languages that a person can learn. Machine language is the most elementary form of programming. This is a string of bits, or binary digits, of zeroes and ones. The 0 stands for no electric pulse, and 1 stands for an electric pulse. The string of electric signals in a certain configuration is the most basic language a computer can understand.

Assembly language is another low-level language that is a little easier to use than machine language, but it is also very limiting. High-level languages are specialized based on how they will be used. Some are based on algebraic formulas and used for solving math and statistics problems. BASIC is one programming language. It is an acronym for Beginners All-Purpose Symbolic Instruction Code. FORTRAN, or Formula Translation, is another program based on algebraic formula. Languages for business data processing include COBOL, or Common Business Oriented Language. Programs that divide objects into different orientations include Java and C++. For building Windows-based applications, it helps to know programs such as Visual Basic, Visual Java, or Visual C.

READING MANUALS

If you are unable to find a college or high school-level course in a digital technology subject that interests you, you can always take the bull by the horns and educate yourself with the help of manuals and online tutorials. Reading a print or online manual can help you quickly and thoroughly learn the ins and outs of a computer, its hardware, its programs, and its operating systems. You can learn it simply for your own enjoyment or to become familiar with the finer points so that you can teach someone else how to master his or her computer system and its capabilities.

Computer courses can be expensive and so can purchasing computer manuals. Check your local library to see if it has computer manuals that can be checked out and read at home. You may find that it has older manuals but not the newest ones you are looking for. Check online to see if you can download an electronic version of the manual you want or watch a tutorial about the program you wish to work with. Even people who feel that they know a computer program pretty well may be surprised by the shortcuts and extra information they can learn from a manual or tutorial.

Even computer-savvy teens can benefit from classes in programming, design, or other formal computer training.

TREND SPOTTING

Even the biggest computer moguls in the world have to keep up with the latest technological developments and newest consumer trends. Every day new technologies are being developed and new products are being released. Keeping up with new tools and trends is crucial if you plan on having a career in computer and digital technology. If you do not keep learning about new technologies as a teen, your knowledge and expertise will quickly become dated. By the time you graduate from college and set out on your career, you will—in technological time—be at least one generation behind.

Computer careers involve constant, lifelong learning. By the time you feel comfortable with a new program, an update or a new version is already available. If you are the type of person who embraces change and is an "early adopter" of new technologies and digital gadgets, you will thrive in the digital technology field. If you are teaching people how to use their computers or providing IT-style assistance to clients, it is essential to be up-to-date. This way you can do your job well and inform clients of new technologies they need to be aware of in order for their businesses to be as efficient as possible, satisfy and expand their customer base, and maintain a competitive edge.

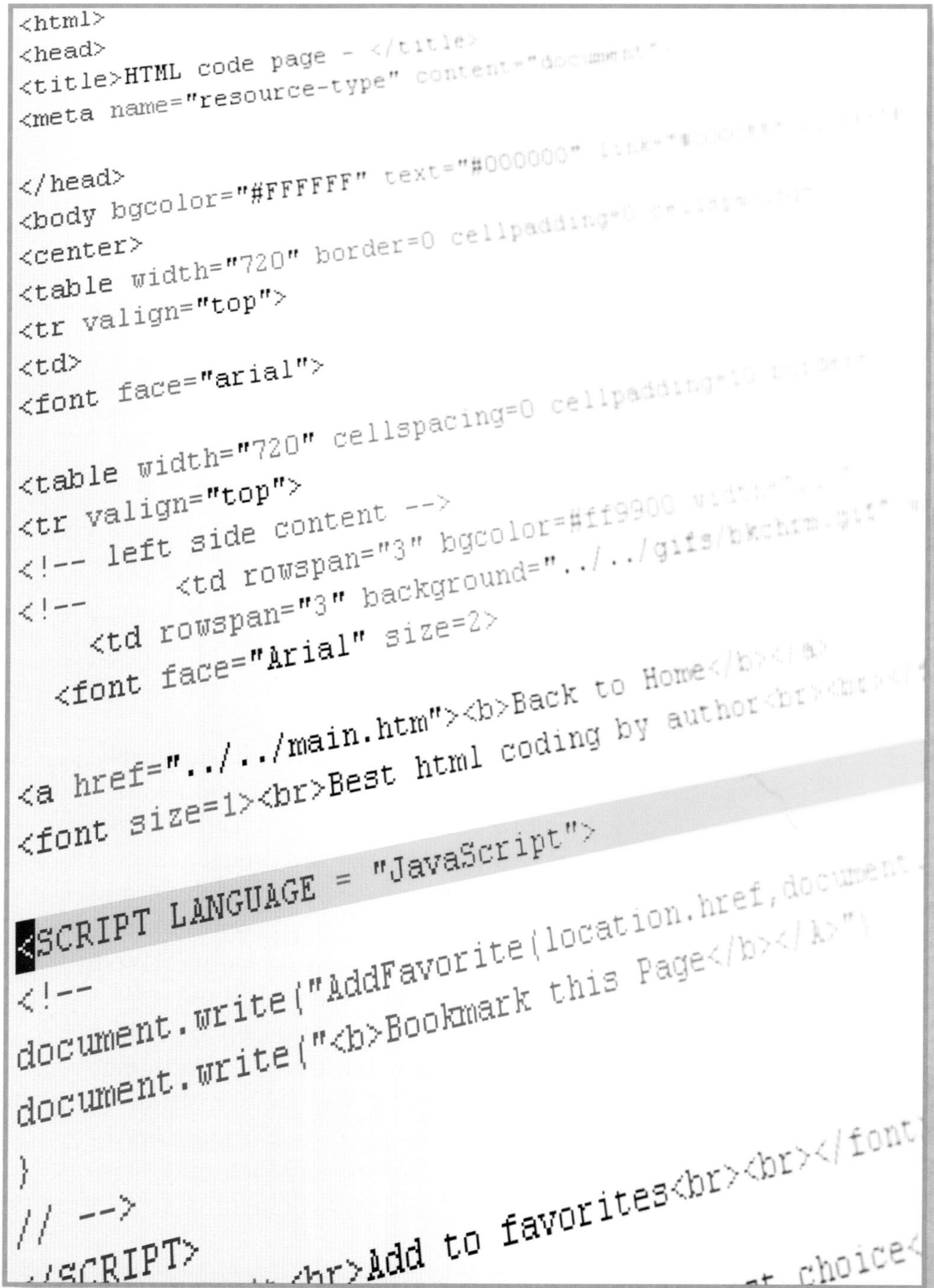
<html>
<head>
<title>HTML code page -
<meta name="resource-type"
</head>
<body bgcolor="#FFFFFF" text="#000000"
<center>
<table width="720" border=0
<tr valign="top">
<td>
<font face="arial">
<table width="720" cellspacing=0
<tr valign="top">
<!-- left side content -->
<!-- <td rowspan="3" bgcolor=
<!-- <td rowspan="3" background="../../
<font face="Arial" size=2>
<a href="../../main.htm"><b>Back to Home
<font size=1>
Best html coding by author
<SCRIPT LANGUAGE = "JavaScript">
<!--
document.write("AddFavorite(location.href,
document.write("<b>Bookmark this Page
}
// -->
</SCRIPT>
Add to favorites

</font
choice

Keeping up-to-date on computer programming or other changing aspects of the computer industry can give you a competitive edge if you are looking for a job in the future. Being able to program—rather than simply being able to use existing computer programs—can give you a huge competitive edge over other job applicants or computer services providers.

STARTING OR JOINING CLUBS

What better way to feel at home than by meeting up with like-minded people? If you are interested in starting your own business or somehow making money with computers, join up with other people who are interested in the same thing and form a club. Computer and entrepreneur clubs are a great place to connect with others who share your digital and money-making interests. Connecting with like-minded people can help ideas flow, energies be harnessed, plans be realized, and goals met. You may even find a potential business partner!

CHOOSING THE RIGHT PATH

Many people who work in the computer field, such as programmers and computer engineers, have at least a bachelor's degree in computer science. There are schools that specialize in this major and offer excellent courses to teach you the basics and keep you up-to-date on the latest technologies and news in the field. However, this may not be necessary. Many community colleges and trade and technical schools also offer great computer training courses.

Remember, however, that a formal academic education is not the only course of action. To some employers and clients, a college degree may not be as important in the field of computers as are practical knowledge and hands-on experience. General know-how and proof that you can do the job may be all that you need. Using a good portfolio to accurately and fully represent your abilities and accomplishments to employers, and showing in an interview that you know about all of the tasks you would be asked to perform on the job, will help you land a job. And it's that job that will start you on a lifelong journey of making money with computers.

Palo Alto, California, is in the heart of Silicon Valley, an area where many high-tech companies are located. Teens in this area have started clubs for entrepreneurs and "tech heads,"

Partnering with other computer-savvy teens is a great way to enhance the strength, creativity, and reach of your efforts when starting an entrepreneurial project or exploring business opportunities.

spawning new apps and start-up companies. The clubs meets to discuss new ventures and ideas, and they talk about ways they can raise money to support their endeavors. They even have high-profile industry guests come in to speak about their experiences starting up companies and implementing their own computer projects.

A group like this can offer great opportunities to brainstorm ideas and develop projects and products. Whether your efforts make money now or down the road does not matter, as long as you are considering the big picture and thinking like an entrepreneur.

GET CLOSE TO THE STARS

The great thing about teen entrepreneur clubs is that they have plenty of local businesses to present their ideas to. When you are geographically close to the companies you want to impress with your business ideas, you have an advantage over those who are not near a hotbed of computer activity.

Silicon Valley is home to Apple, Hewlett-Packard, Intel, Cisco Systems, Oracle, Google, Yahoo!, Adobe Systems, and dozens of other companies that specialize in computer and Internet technology.

This student works on microchips at an academy that provides high-tech start-up companies and entrepreneurs with the digital equipment, tools, and resources necessary to test their ideas and refine their innovative products.

Some adults, determined to work for one of these computer giants, relocate to the area and work for smaller but similar companies first, in hopes of some day switching jobs and going to work for one of the industry's top ten companies. Some people feel that living in a place surrounded by so many other like-minded people will benefit them by making it easier to find a potential business partner, financial backer, and network of influential contacts.

You don't have to go all the way to Silicon Valley to make a splash in the computer world, however. You can do that right in your own community if you have the right ideas and the determination to make your dreams come true. If you truly want to make money now by using your computer skills, you can find a way to make it happen.

GLOSSARY

APP Short for "application," a computer program or software meant to fulfill a particular purpose.

ASSEMBLY LANGUAGE A low-level programming language that is used in intercomputer communication.

BASIC An algebraic-based computer language that stands for "Beginners All-Purpose Symbolic Instruction Code."

BINARY A system of numerical communication, such as a string of zeroes and ones.

COMPUTER ENGINEER A person who develops computer systems and analyzes software.

CONSULTANT A person who works on a project basis—rather than as a full-time employee—for a company.

DATABASE A structured set of data that is accessible by many people.

ENTREPRENEUR A person who develops, organizes, and operates a new business venture.

ETHICS Moral principles that govern the way a person acts, including in business situations.

FORTRAN A high-level computer language based in algebraic formulas, standing for "Formula Translation."

INTERNSHIP A student trainee who works, often without pay, to gain experience in a given field.

IT DEPARTMENT The information technology department at a company, dealing with systematizing, operating, and maintaining the company's computer network and systems and training employees to use company computers, programs, and other relevant digital technologies.

JAVA A high-level computer language that divides objects into different orientations.

MACHINE LANGUAGE The most elementary form of programming, using strings of binary digits to communicate.

MENTOR An experienced and trusted adviser who assists in one's academic and professional education and advancement.

PORTFOLIO A physical or virtual archive of samples of a person's work that, when displayed, demonstrates that person's range, skill, and accomplishment in his or her field of endeavor.

PROGRAMMING The action or process of writing computer programs.

RÉSUMÉ A brief listing or summary of a person's education, professional experience, and qualifications.

SILICON VALLEY The name given to an area of California that has a high concentration of computer and Internet technology companies.

TEMPORARY AGENCY A service that fills a corporation's need for temporary employees with the right people who can perform the required job.

FOR MORE INFORMATION

Association for Experiential Education (AEE)
3775 Iris Avenue, Suite #4
Boulder, CO 80301-2043
(303) 440-8844
Web site: http://www.aee.org
AEE is a nonprofit, professional membership association dedicated
to experiential education and the students, educators, and
practitioners who use its philosophy.

Canada Summer Jobs
Service Canada
Canada Enquiry Centre
Ottawa, ON K1A OJ9
Canada
(800) 935-5555
Web site: http://www.servicecanada.gc.ca/eng/epb/yi/yep/pro-
grams/scpp.shtml
Canada Summer Jobs is a government-funded program to help
employers create summer job opportunities for students.

Computers for Youth (CFY)
520 Eighth Avenue, Floor 25
New York, NY 10018
(212) 563-7300
Web site: http://cfy.org
CFY is a national nonprofit organization that helps students, teach-
ers, and parents use digital learning to improve educational
outcomes. It improves the home learning environment of
four thousand low-income middle school students and their

families by providing them with a home computer, top-notch educational software in core subject areas, Internet access, tech support, and family workshops designed to increase parents' confidence as learning partners for their children.

Discovery Internships

134 West 26th Street, Suite 1200
New York, NY 10001
(212) 367-5695
Web site: http://www.highschoolinternships.com/high-school
Discovery Internships provides customized internship programs for high school students.

DoSomething.org

19 West 21st Street, 8th Floor
New York, NY 10010
(212) 254-2390
Web site: http://www.Dosomething.org
This organization is dedicated to social change and accepts interns who are committed self-starters, including tech wizard interns.

Dream Careers

2221 Broadway Street
Redwood City, CA 94063
(800) 251-2933
Web site: http://www.summerinternships.com
Dream Careers provides summer internship opportunities in the film industry for college students.

Federal Student Work Experience Program (FSWEP)

Service Canada
Canada Enquiry Centre

Ottawa, ON K1A OJ9
Canada
(800) 532-9397
Web site: http://www.servicecanada.gc.ca/eng/goc/fswep
.shtml
This government-funded program is designed to match student skills
with various departments and agencies of government.

Fund for Social Entrepreneurs
Youth Service America
1101 15th Street, Suite 200
Washington, DC 20005
Web site: http://www.servenet.org
This organization provides financial support to youth groups inter-
ested in entrepreneurial endeavors.

Internship Institute
2865 South Eagle Road
Newtown, PA 18940
(215) 870-9700
Web site: http://www.internshipinstitute.org
The Internship Institute is a nonprofit, nonpartisan organization
whose mission is to assure the quality, integrity, and success of
internships in order for individuals, organizations, and econo-
mies to prosper. It is the only nonprofit solely dedicated to the
advancement of best practices globally through education,
collaboration, and advocacy.

Junior Achievement
One Education Way
Colorado Springs, CO 80906
(719) 540-8000
Web site: http://www.ja.org
This volunteer-based group is dedicated to educating young people
about business and economics education.

The KidsWay Inc.
P.O. Box 7987
Atlanta, GA 30357-9911
(888) KIDSWAY (543-7929)
Web site: http://www.kidsway.com
KidsWay fosters the entrepreneurial development of young people
  ages eight to eighteen.

Media Job Search Canada
1403 Royal York Road, Suite 608
Toronto, ON M9P 0A1
Canada
(416) 651-5111
Web site: http://www.mediajobsearchcanada.com
This is a job search service for Canadians interested in jobs in the
  media.

U.S. Department of Labor
Frances Perkins Building
200 Constitution Avenue NW
Washington, DC 20210
(866) 4-USA-DOL (1-866-487-2365)
Web site: http://www.dol.gov
The Department of Labor's mission is to foster, promote, and develop
  the welfare of the wage earners, job seekers, and retirees of the
  United States; improve working conditions; advance opportunities for profitable employment; and assure work-related
  benefits and rights.

VolunteerMatch
717 California Street, 2nd Floor
San Francisco, CA 94108
(415) 241-6868

VolunteerMatch strengthens communities by making it easier for good people and good causes to connect. The organization offers a variety of online services to support a community of nonprofit, volunteer, and business leaders committed to civic engagement. Its popular service welcomes millions of visitors a year and has become the preferred Internet recruiting tool for more than eighty-one thousand nonprofit organizations.

YouthLearn Education Development Center
43 Foundry Avenue
Waltham, MA 02453-8313
(800) 449-5525
The YouthLearn Initiative offers youth development professionals and educators comprehensive services and resources for using media and technology tools to create exciting learning environments.

WEB SITES

Due to the changing nature of Internet links, Rosen Publishing has developed an online list of Web sites related to the subject of this book. This site is updated regularly. Please use this link to access the list:

http://www.rosenlinks.com/MMN/Comp

FOR FURTHER READING

Cinnamon, Ian. *Programming Video Games for the Evil Genius*. New York, NY: McGraw-Hill/TAB Electronics, 2008.

Dawson, Michael. *Beginning C++ Through Game Programming*. Boston, MA: Course Technology PTR, 2007.

Dille, Flint. *The Ultimate Guide to Video Game Writing and Design*. Los Angeles, CA: Lone Eagle, 2008.

Duggan, Michael. *Torque for Teens*. Boston, MA: Course Technology PTR, 2010.

Duggan, Michael. *2D Game Building for Teens*. Boston, MA: Course Technology PTR, 2011.

Duggan, Michael. *Wii Game Creation for Teens*. Boston, MA: Course Technology PTR, 2010.

Farrell, Mary. *Computer Programming for Teens*. Boston, MA: Course Technology PTR, 2007.

Ferguson Publishing Company. *Discovering Careers for Your Future: Environment*. New York, NY: Ferguson, 2008.

Ford, Jerry Lee, Jr. *Scratch Programming for Teens*. Boston, MA: Course Technology PTR, 2008.

Fryer, Julie. *The Teen's Ultimate Guide to Making Money When You Can't Get a Job: 199 Ideas for Earning Cash on Your Own Terms*. Ocala, FL: Atlantic Publishing Group, 2012.

Ham, Ethan. *The Building Blocks of Game Design*. New York, NY: Routledge, 2013.

Harbour, Jonathan S. *Visual Basic Game Programming for Teens.* Boston, MA: Course Technology PTR, 2010.

Harbour, Jonathan S. *Visual C# Game Programming for Teens.* Boston, MA: Course Technology PTR, 2010.

Hardnett, Charles. *Programming Like a Pro for Teens.* Boston, MA: Course Technology PTR, 2011.

Hardnett, Charles. *Virtual World Design and Creation for Teens.* Boston, MA: Course Technology PTR, 2009.

Keller, Debra. *Creating 2D Animation with Adobe CS6.* New York, NY: Delmar Cengage Learning, 2013.

Labovich, Laura M., and Miriam Salpeter. *100 Conversations for Career Success: Learn to Network, Cold Call, and Tweet Your Way to Your Dream Job.* New York, NY: Learning Express, 2012.

Love, Paul E. *Find an IT Job: Information Technology Careers from Bioinformatics to Web Design.* Seattle, WA: CreateSpace, 2012.

McDowell, Gayle Laakmann. *The Google Resume: How to Prepare for a Career and Land a Job at Apple, Microsoft, Google, or Any Top Tech Company.* Hoboken, NJ: Wiley, 2011.

Misner, Ivan, et al. *Networking Like a Pro: Turning Contacts into Connections.* Irvine, CA: Entrepreneur Press, 2010.

Mureta, Chad. *App Empire: Make Money, Have a Life, and Let Technology Work for You.* Hoboken, NJ: Wiley, 2012.

Murphy, Mary. *Beginner's Guide to Animation: Everything You Need to Know to Get Started.* New York, NY: Watson Guptill, 2008.

Rogers, Scott. *Level Up!: The Guide to Great Video Game Design*. Hoboken, NJ: Wiley, 2010.

Sande, Warren, and Carter Sande. *Hello World! Computer Programming for Kids and Other Beginners*. Greenwich, CT: Manning Publications, 2009.

Selfridge, Benjamin, and Peter Selfridge. *A Teen's Guide to Creating Web Pages and Blogs*. Waco, TX: Prufrock Press, 2008.

Sethi, Maneesh. *Game Programming for Teens*. Boston, MA: Course Technology PTR, 2008.

Sethi, Maneesh. *3D Game Programming for Teens*. Boston, MA: Course Technology PTR, 2009.

Sethi, Maneesh. *Web Design for Teens*. Boston, MA: Course Technology PTR, 2004.

Wyatt, Andy. *The Complete Digital Animation Course: Principles, Practices, and Techniques: A Practical Guide for Aspiring Animators*. Hauppauge, NY: Barron's Educational Series, 2010.

Yarmosh, Ken, and John Jantsch. *App Savvy: Turning Ideas into iPad and iPhone Apps Customers Really Want*. Sebastopol, CA: O'Reilly Media, 2010.

BIBLIOGRAPHY

Adobe Photoshop. "Lightroom Killer Tips." Retrieved August 2012 (http://lightroomkillertips.com).

MercuryNews.com. "Apple's Big Year Outshines Mixed Result for Silicon Valley." 2012. Retrieved August 2012 (http://www.mercurynews.com/sv150).

Baird, Leslie B. "Summer Jobs for Teens Working with Computers." Helium.com, July 22, 2010. Retrieved August 2012 (http://www.helium.com/items/1900365-summer-jobs-for-teens-with-computer-skills).

Bennington, Emily, and Skip Lineberg. *Effective Immediately: How to Fit In, Stand Out, and Move Up at Your First Real Job*. New York, NY: Ten Speed Press, 2010.

Berger, Lauren. *All Work, No Pay: Finding an Internship, Building Your Resume, Making Connections, and Gaining Job Experience*. Berkeley, CA: Ten Speed Press, 2012.

Berger, Rob. "8 Lucrative Business Ideas for High School Students." DoughRoller.com. Retrieved August 2012 (http://www.doughroller.net/personal-finance/high-paying-jobs-for-high-school-students).

Berger, Sandra. *Ultimate Guide to Summer Opportunities for Teens: 200 Programs That Prepare You for College Success*. Waco, TX: Prufrock Press, 2007.

Biography.com. "Mark Zuckerberg." Retrieved August 2012 (http://www.biography.com/people/mark-zuckerberg-507402).

Boles, Blake. *Better Than College: How to Build a Successful Life Without a Four-Year Degree.* Springfield, OR: Tells Peak Press, 2012.

Campbell, Nicole. "Careers in the Computer Industry." eHow. Retrieved August 2012 (http://www.ehow.com/about_5398557_careers-computer-industry.html).

Cheney, Alexandra. "Kid Entrepreneurs Build iPhone App." Inc.com, July 1, 2009. Retrieved August 2012 (http://www.inc.com/news/articles/2009/07/iphone-app.html).

Doyle, Alison. "Work at Home Scams: Avoiding Job and Work at Home Scams." About.com. Retrieved August 2012 (http://jobsearch.about.com/cs/workathomehelp/a/homescam.htm).

Ferguson Publishing Company. *Discovering Careers for Your Future: Environment.* New York, NY: Ferguson, 2008.

Fryer, Julie. *The Teen's Ultimate Guide to Making Money When You Can't Get a Job: 199 Ideas for Earning Cash on Your Own Terms.* Ocala, FL: Atlantic Publishing Group, 2012.

Gadara, Chirag. "Online Jobs for Teenagers—No Experience or Investment Required." GuideToEarnMoney.com, January 27, 2011. Retrieved August 2012 (http://www.guidetoearnmoney.com/data-entry-jobs/online-jobs-for-teenagers-no-experience-or-investment-required-part-1.html).

Hardy, Quentin "Doing Apps and Start-Ups While Still in High School." *New York Times*, July 2, 2012. Retrieved August 2012 (http://www.nytimes.com/2012/07/03/technology/palo-alto-high-club-fosters-would-be-tech-moguls.html?_r=1&hpw).

Hub Pages. "Types of Computer Languages with their Advantages and Disadvantages." Retrieved August 2012 (http://ninjacraze.hubpages.com/hub/Types-of-Computer-Languages-with-Advantages-and-Disadvantages).

Internships.com. "IT/Computer Technology Internships." Retrieved August 2012 (http://www.internships.com/intern/it).

James, Justin. "10 Things You Have to Know to Be Computer Literate." *Tech Republic*, February 6, 2012. Retrieved August 2012 (http://www.techrepublic.com/blog/10things/10-things-you-have-to-know-to-be-computer-literate/3028).

Lagorio, Christine. "How to Make Money on iPhone Apps." Inc.com, March 12, 2010. Retrieved August 2012 (http://www.inc.com/guides/making-money-iphone-apps.html).

Lehman, Jeff. *First Job—First Paycheck: How to Get the Most Out of Both Without Help from Your Parents*. Seattle, WA: Mentor Press, LLC, 2011.

Mandell, Nancy R. "5 Summer Tax Tips for Working Teens." *Reuters Money*, June 22, 2011. Retrieved August 2012 (http://blogs.reuters.com/reuters-money/2011/06/22/5-summer-tax-tips-for-working-teens).

Misner, Ivan, et al. *Networking Like a Pro: Turning Contacts into Connections*. Irvine, CA: Entrepreneur Press, 2010.

Misner, Ivan, and Michelle R. Donovan. *The 29% Solution: 52 Weekly Networking Success Strategies*. Austin, TX: Greenleaf Book Group Press, 2008.

Swearingen, Jake. "Social Networking for Business." *CBS Money Watch*, September 5, 2008. Retrieved August 2012 (http://

www.cbsnews.com/8301-505125_162-51219914/social
-networking-for-business).

Thelin, Nicole. "Labor Laws for Teens." eHow. Retrieved August
2012 (http://www.ehow.com/about_5125665_labor-laws
-teens.html).

U.S. Department of Labor. "Youth and Labor Age Requirements."
Retrieved August 2012 (http://www.dol.gov/dol/topic
/youthlabor/agerequirements.htm).

Vohwinkle, Jeremy. "Jobs for Teens to Make Money." About
.com. Retrieved August 2012 (http://financialplan.about
.com/od/students/a/Jobs-For-Teens-To-Make-Money.htm).

INDEX

ABOUT THE AUTHOR

Kathy Furgang has been an author for Rosen for many years, writing books about the Internet, digital animation, careers, and the economy. She lives in upstate New York with her husband and two sons, who all enjoy being computer savvy.

PHOTO CREDITS

Cover Goodluz/Shutterstock.com; pp. 5, 26–27, 46–47, 48 iStockphoto/Thinkstock; p. 8 © iStockphoto.com/Andrew Howe; p. 9 Sima/Shutterstock.com; p. 11 Jupiterimages/Comstock/Thinkstock; pp. 14–15 © Brigette Sullivan/PhotoEdit; pp. 16–17, 39, 60–61 © AP Images; p. 19 Supri Suharjoto/Shutterstock.com; pp. 22–23 Bloomberg/Getty Images; p. 24 Clerkenwell/the Agency Collection/Getty Images; pp. 28–29 Goodshoot/Thinkstock; pp. 32–33 Garsya/Shutterstock.com; p. 34 Brendan O'Sullivan/Photolibrary/Getty Images; pp. 36–37 Stephen Coburn/Shutterstock.com; pp. 40–41 Joselito Briones/the Agency Collection/Getty Images; pp. 44–45 © The U-T San Diego/ZUMA Press; p. 50 Ableimages/Photodisc/Getty Images; pp. 54–55 Jetta Productions/Lifesize/Getty Images; p. 56 nasirkhan/Shutterstock.com; pp. 58–59 Jupiterimages/Brand X Pictures/Thinkstock; pp. 3–5, 62–80 (background image), page borders, boxed text backgrounds © iStockphoto.com/Tomasz Sowinski; back cover and remaining interior background image © iStockphoto.com/Pavel Khorenyan.

Designer: Brian Garvey; Photo Researcher: Karen Huang